INVESTORS GET RICH

Learn year 2015 trend in stock market

Learn fundamental factors of investing

Read the Book and Profit

Knowledge is power

BASKER SELWYN

Legal Disclaimer

This book contains general information regarding finance and investment that is based on the author's own knowledge and experience. It is published for general reference and it is not intended to be substituted for the advice of a financial professional or accountant. The publisher and the author disclaim any personal liability either directly or indirectly for the information contained within.

The strategies outlined in this book may not be suitable for every individual and not guaranteed or warranted to produce any particular result. This book does not represent a recommendation to buy or sell or hold any security.

Although the author and the publisher have made every effort to ensure the accuracy and completeness of the information presented here, they assume no responsibility for errors in accuracies, omissions and inconsistencies.

None of the contents contained in this book should be considered as investment advice. Investors should speak with their financial advisors for any investment advice and discuss the risk of investing in any financial products.

Copyright

Copyright@2014 Basker Selwyn All rights reserved
No part of this book may be reproduced or transmitted in any form or by any means or stored in a database retrieval system without the prior written permission of the publisher.

ISBN 13: 978 1502716842
ISBN 10: 1502716844

Table of contents

1. Introduction — 1
2. investors — 2
3. Economy — 5
4. Money Supply — 7
5. Jobless claim report — 8
6. Retail Sales Report — 9
7. Consumer price index — 10
8. Gross Domestic Product — 11
9. Purchasing Managers Index — 12
10. Factory Order Report — 13
11. Durable Goods Report — 14
12. New Residential Housing Construction Report — 15
13. Existing Home Sales Report — 15
14. Mutual Fund flow — 16

15. Interest rate	17
16. Beige Book	18
17. Terrorist Incidents	19
18. Recession	19
19. Depression	20
20. Bull Market	21
21. Bear Market	22
22. Federal Reserve Monetary Policy	23
23. Stock Market Indexes	24
a) Dow Jones Industrial Average Index	24
b) S&P 500 Index	26
c) Nasdaq Composite index	50
d) Nasdaq 100 index	50
24. Brokerage Firms in the United States	56
25. Stock Market in the year 2015- Conclusion	61

Investors get rich

INTRODUCTION

Investors get rich. If investors invest in any investment at the right time, have patients and discipline they gain financially. Most of the rich people in any country invested their money in any kind of investment like stocks, bonds, real estate, small businesses , currencies and commodities at the right time.

This book is written for investors who want to invest in the stock market for long term. This book is for investors who have patients and discipline.

This book is mainly about the general stock market trend in the year 2015.

It gives investors the knowledge how they should calculate risks and rewards when investing in the stock market. The book is precise and explains how the investors should take action (buy, sell or hold)in certain conditions in the economy of the country.

It explains what economic indicators the investors should look for when investing in stock market. It explains the fundamental reasons why the stock market goes up or down. It is a book simple to understand and read. It is helpful for investors worldwide.

Basker Selwyn

INVESTORS

Investor is a person who set apart funds to invest in different kinds of investments with the expectation of financial gains. There are many kinds of investments. But the popular investments are

1.**STOCKS (equity)**

Share in the ownership of a corporation or stake in a company. If the price of the stock goes up the investors in that company gain their capital. But if the stock goes down the investors in that company loses their capital. When you own a stock of a company you are a part owner of that corporation. Over the long run stocks outperform bonds. Stock has made lot of people wealthy.
Investors in the stock market should know when to buy and when to sell the stocks. They should also know what price they should pay for the stocks. Investors in the stocks should have patients and discipline when they are investing in stocks.

Investors get rich

2. BONDS

When you invest in bonds you become a banker. You are a lender to the companies or others. When United States Government, Companies, Counties or municipalities want money to be raised they offer bond. That is the way they raise money other than raising taxes or prices. Investing in bonds does not make you owner of the corporation as in the case of stocks.

3. REAL ESTATE

Real Estate is immovable properties like land, commercial buildings, houses and apartments. Real estate is one of the major investment opportunities available to the investors. This industry has also made lot of people wealthy. People can make money by developing the properties, flipping the properties, renting and managing the apartment buildings.

4. SMALL BUSINESSES

Investing in small businesses is a great opportunity for investors who want financial freedom. Investors can own their own restaurants, gas stations, dry cleaning store hotels, motels or sporting goods store.

5. CURRENCY

It is the monetary units in different countries. The example for currency is the U.S. dollars, British pounds and Euros. The value of the currency of a nation changes constantly. Traders trade on the belief that a country's currency goes up or down. It is traded in the foreign exchange markets. The forex market is considered the largest market for currencies in the world.

6. COMMODITIES

Individual investors can invest in commodities like gold, crude oil, cotton, wheat, coffee, cocoa and sugar.
If they make investment in the right commodity at the right time and right price they can financially gain. Chicago Board of trade is the major commodity exchange in the United States.

As you know all the investments have risks and rewards. In this book we are going to concentrate on investment in the stock market and various economic indicators while investing.

Investors get rich

ECONOMY

Investment decisions can not only be made by individual company earnings, cash flow, sales and net profit. The investors should look for various economic indicators that are important in making investment decisions. The return for your investment depends on how you act in certain economic conditions.

If you make the right decision to buy or sell in the stock market, you gain your capital. If you make the wrong decision to buy or sell, you lose your capital

Stocks gain on positive economic data and outlook. Corporations or companies earn more profit if the country's economy is growing .The prospects for growth is good.

Stock market falls on news of terrorist attacks in any part of the world. Political instability can also cause economic instability and the stocks fall.

Economy in other countries also affects the economy in a particular country. For example when the economies in European countries are down the United States cannot sell goods to those countries. This eventually affects the economy of the United States. This will cause the stocks to fall.

Basker Selwyn

Stock market rise when the economies of other nations do well. For example if the Asian country's economy is doing better they buy more products from the United States. That will create more jobs here in the United States and consequently the stock market will rise.

The world economies are interconnected. The United States, China, Japan, Germany and France have the large economies in the world as of year 2014.
We can find from the different economic indicators what the economy is doing. The main indicators are
1. Money Supply Report
2. Jobless Claims Report
3. Retail sales Report
4. Consumer price Index
5. Gross Domestic Product Index
6. Purchasing Managers Index
7. Factory Orders Report
8. Durable Goods Report
9. New Residential Housing Construction Report
10. Existing Home Sales Report
11. Mutual Fund Flow
12. Interest Rate
13. Beige book report

Investors get rich

MONEY SUPPLY REPORT

The money supply report is released by Federal Reserve Board. It is released every Thursday of the week in the United States.

Interest rates are lowered by supply of more money. This result in more investments and the consumer has more money in their hands. This stimulates the economy and the business activity thereby raising the demand for labor. This will increase the stock prices.

If the money supply declines the interest rate will be higher and the investments in business will be less.
This results in less money in the hands of consumers. The Business activity will be diminished lowering the demand for labor. The stocks will fall in this situation.

It provides the measures of the monetary aggregates (M1 and M2) and their components . M1 and M2 are progressively more inclusive measures of money.
M1 is included in M2.

Federal Reserve has control over the money supply. Through its daily course of business the Federal Reserve changes the money supply.

Basker Selwyn

JOBLESS CLAIMS REPORT

Investors in stock market should have an eye on the unemployment rate report. This report shows the health of the economy in a country.

More people with jobs will result in higher economic growth. The savings for individuals increases. As a result retail sales will grow. So the corporate profit increases with decrease in unemployment rate. People are willing to spend money when they have job. Ultimately the stock prices will rise.

If the report shows less people with jobs then it will result in lower economic growth. The savings for individuals decreases. As a result retail sales will decline. So the corporate profit decreases with increase in unemployment rate. People are not willing to spend money when they do not have job. Eventually the stock prices will fall.

The United States Department of labor releases the weekly jobless claims report. The stock prices fluctuate according to the report. In September 2014 the unemployment rate is 5.9% in the United States.

Investors get rich

RETAIL SALES REPORT

Investors watch country's retail sales to determine the economy is doing well. The Retail Sales Report is released by the United States Department of Commerce. The report is released by the middle of each month.

Retail Sales Report includes the Auto sales, general merchandise sales, furniture, electronics, building material, Food , beverage, health, personal care, clothing ,sporting goods, hobby ,book and music store sales.

Retail Sales Report compares sales in last month and last year in the same period. The annual retail sales report is also released annually around March of every year.

The United States Department of commerce release quarterly retail E commerce Sales report every quarter. If the Retail sales report shows growth in sales comparatively to the previous month and previous year the investors are optimistic about the economy of the country and ultimately the stock prices will rise. If the Retail sales report shows decline in the sales from previous month and previous year the investors are pessimistic and the stock price will fall.

Basker Selwyn

CONSUMER PRICE INDEX (CPI)

The prices of goods and services to consumers are measured by this index called consumer price index.

Department of labor statistics releases this index. It is a popular indicator of the economy in the country.

The index tracks the inflation and deflation in the country. If the inflation increases by 2% the consumer price index will increase by 2%. If the deflation increased by 1%, the consumer price index will decrease by 1%.

If the consumer price index goes too much higher, it is time to get out of the stock market. Federal Reserve set the monetary policy according to the consumer price index.

The consumer price index (CPI) is released monthly And it covers the previous month figures.

Investors get rich

GROSS DOMESTIC PRODUCT

The United States Department of Commerce Bureau of Economic Analysis reports the Gross Domestic Product growth in the country.

Gross domestic product is the total dollar value of all goods and services produces in certain time frame. It is the total size of the economy. The United States has one of the largest economy in the world. The United States has about 17 trillion dollars in Gross Domestic Product in the year 2014. China has about 10 trillion dollars in Gross Domestic Product in the year 2014.

adjusted annual rate. It is compared to the previous quarter growth also. The report includes the import,
Export, consumer spending and corporate profits (financial and non-financial)

In the United States the Gross Domestic Product growth for the second quarter of 2014 was 4%. Retail, wholesale health care, real estate rental and leasing were up. They contributed for more than 50% of the total Gross Domestic Product growth.

There is a relationship between stock market returns and Gross Domestic Product expectation. The stocks go up when the GDP growth is expected and realized.

Basker Selwyn

PURCHASING MANAGER INDEX

Purchasing Manager Index is released by the Markit financial information services Group and Institute for supply Management. The report is released monthly.

The Markit survey provides survey for more than 30 countries. It provides Purchasing Manager Index report over 400 companies. It provides information about the health of the economy, inflation, exports, employment and inventories. It covers the manufacturing sector and services sector.

From 1948 the institute for supply management started reporting this index in the United States. It consists of report on businesses, manufacturing data and nonmanufacturing data.

Generally the PMI above 50 indicates that the economy is expanding. If the PMI is below 50 the economy is contracting. It will affect the Gross Domestic Product growth and ultimately the economy. The investors can figure out the recession is near or not looking the PMI report.

Investors get rich

FACTORY ORDERS REPORT

Factory orders report is released by the United States Census Bureau. It is released usually within 10th of every month. It includes durable and non- durable goods new orders for factories in the country. The report consists of new orders for durable goods like airplane, cars and machineries.

The report also shows the new orders for non-durable items like food and apparel. It is useful for the investors to know what the trend is in the manufacturing sector. The Gross Domestic Product growth can be known by the investors.

More durable and non- durable goods are ordered when the economy is improving. This shows the Gross domestic Product growth is up. That means the stocks are going up.

Less durable and non-durable goods are ordered when the economy is declining. This shows the Gross domestic product growth is down. This will result in stock market fall.

Basker Selwyn

DURABLE GOODS REPORT

The Durable Goods Report is released by the United States Census Bureau. It is released about middle of every month. The businesses order more durable goods when the economy improves. This shows the Gross Domestic Product growth. It is favorable for the stock market.

Less domestic goods are ordered when the economy is declining. That will result in Gross Domestic Product Decline and the stocks will go down. It may create recession.

Industrial production can be measure by this indicator. Durable goods are the capital goods like air planes, cars and machinery. It shows the manufacturing activity growth. The data is collected from more than 4000 durable goods manufacturers.

Investors get rich

NEW RESIDENTIAL HOUSING CONSTRUCTION REPORT

The new residential housing construction report is published by the United States Census Bureau. It is released middle of the month. The report shows three elements namely housing starts, building permits and housing completions. The report is divided into four regions namely north east, Midwest, south, and west. Investors can use this indicator as a supportive indicator to the other reports. If the interest rate increases the housing starts will show no progress.

EXISTING HOME SALES REPORT

Existing home sales report is published by National Association of Realtors. It is released last week of the month. The report compares the previous period. It includes the sales of single family homes, townhomes, condominiums and co-ops.

If the report shows rise in the sales then the economy is in good shape. If the report shows decline in the existing home sales then it means the economy is in bad shape. Investors look for this indicator to invest in the stock market.

Basker Selwyn

MUTUAL FUND FLOWS REPORT

Mutual fund flows report is released by Investment Company Institute. It covers stocks, bonds and money market. Investment company institute represents United States Mutual funds, United States unit investment trusts, United States exchange traded funds, United States Closed End Funds and Undertaking for collective investment in transferable securities fund.

The demand in stocks and bonds are reported in this indicator. The investor can decide whether he has to buy, sell or hold the stocks accordingly.

This indicator shows the investor sentiment and the contrarians use this indicator to trade stocks.

Investors get rich

INTEREST RATE

Corporations make more profit when there is economic growth and lower interest rate. Investors are willing to buy more stocks when the interest rate is lower in the banks. The investors do not want to keep the money in the bank for lower interest. This will result in lower demand for bonds because of lower yield in the bonds. The investors get more returns in the stocks and the stocks rise.

Companies make less profit when there is higher interest rate. The economic growth slows. Investors are not willing to buy stocks when interest rate is high. They can keep the money in the bank for higher interest or buy bonds for more yields. In this case there is less demand for stocks and the stock prices go down.

Federal Reserve determines the interest rate in the nation. It keeps the interest rate lower to grow the economic activity. It helps to get finance for a new home. It also keeps the inflation under control. The Federal Reserve try to keep the unemployment rate lower. Lower interest rate also helps the business to get more finances. It also help for more demand for stocks.

Basker Selwyn

BEIGE BOOK REPORT

Beige book is the report on current economic conditions by Federal Reserve. This report contains information by sector and districts. It is published before the meeting of Federal open market committee. It is released eight times a year and contains interviews with economists and market experts.

It contains reports on the major sectors namely retail, financial services, non-financial services manufacturing, real estate, agriculture, and natural resources.

It shows the reports on various districts namely Boston, New York, Philadelphia , Cleveland, Atlanta, Chicago, St. Louis, Minneapolis, Kansas city, Dallas and San Francisco.

Investors should have an eye on the report to make any decision in investing in the stock market.

Investors get rich

TERRORIST INCIDENTS

Terrorist attacks within the United States and globally affect the stock market. One of the examples is the attack happened on September 11,2001. The attack happened in the morning 8 to 9a.m. The New York Stock Exchange and NASDAQ did not open until September 17th. On the 1st day of trading after 9/11 attack the market fell above 600 points. Many sectors including airline, financial, entertainment, tourism, and hospitality were affected by the attack.

RECESSION

Recession in the country slows down the Gross Domestic Product growth and it makes the economy go down.
The unemployment rate is higher in the time of recession. A large percentage of people do not have job and they do not have money to spend.

The recession makes the stock market to go down.
The real estate market falls down. Many industries like Finance and the Automobile industries are affected because of the recession. Sometimes the Stock Market decline precedes the recession.

Basker Selwyn

DEPRESSION

Depression is one of the reasons for decline in stock market. The real Gross domestic product decreases above 10%. The recession last above two years. These are the two reasons we look for when there is a depression. The economy is in bad shape and the unemployment rate is high in the country when there is Depression.

Great Depression occurred in the year 1929. It lasted until the year 1933 in the United States. It started preceding the World War II. Most of the countries were affected by the depression. The unemployment rate reached above 20%. The Gross Domestic Product was down a lot. Industrial production was lower. The wholesale prices and foreign trade declined. The stock market crash happened on October 29th 1929 called black Tuesday. The United States economy fell down. This affected the other country's economies too. The stock market reached bottom in the year 1933. Most countries started their relief programs. The recovery began in the year 1933. But the full recovery did not happen until 1939.

Investors get rich

BULL MARKET

Bull market occurs when the stock market goes up. Investors are optimistic about the economy and stock market trend is up. The interest rate is low comparatively. The Federal policies are favorable for the stock market. Incidents like terrorist attacks and natural disaster do not happen at time of bull market.

The years when bull markets occurred were

1. from year 1877 to year 1906.
2. from year 1921 to year 1929
3. from year 1949 to year 1968
4. from year 1982 to year 2000
5. from year 2003 to year 2007
6. from year 2009 to present year 2014.

The bull market is still continuing until now in September 2014. The Dow Jones Average index and S&P 500 index are making all-time highs. They both are in record territories as of September 2014.

Basker Selwyn

BEAR MARKET

Bear market occurs when the stock market goes down. The investors are pessimistic about the stock market and the market trend is down. The interest rate is higher comparatively. Incidents like terrorist attacks and natural Disaster can happen at the time bear market.

The years when the bear market occurred were

1. from year 1906 to year 1921
2. from year 1929 to year 1933
3. from year 1937 to year 1949
4. from year 1968 to year 1982
5. from year 2000 to year 2003
6. from year 2007 to year 2008.

Bear market happens at the time of recession and depression. The stock market can go new lows and some-times the stock market crashes at the time of depression and recession.

Investors get rich

FEDERAL RESERVE MONETARY POLICY

The Federal Reserve has the power to raise or lower the interest rate in the country. If the Federal Reserve buys more Government backed securities, the interest rate will decrease. If the Federal Reserve sells more Government backed securities the interest rate will increase.
The Federal Reserve controls the inflation by adjusting the interest rate. This way it controls the employment and the economy of the country. It also regulates the value of the dollar. It controls the money circulation within the country.

The Federal Reserve chairman is appointed by the president and confirmed by the senate. The chairman is the top in the Federal Reserve System. The chairman is one of the seven members of the board of governors.

The present chair of Federal Reserve is
Mrs. Janet Yellen . She assumed office on February 3rd 2014. She is the first woman to hold the position as Federal Chair.

Federal open market committee is the committee within the Federal Reserve System. It makes decisions about the interest rate and the money supply.
Federal Advisory Council advises the Federal Reserve Board .

Basker Selwyn

STOCK MARKET INDEXES

Stock market indexes are created to find out what different Segments in the market are doing. We can tell from the indexes the general market trend.

There are many stock market indexes in the United States. We have listed four of them here in this book.

1. Dow Jones Industrial Average index
2. S&P 500 index
3. Nasdaq composite index
4. Nasdaq 100 stock index

DOW JONES INDUSTRIAL AVERAGE

It is called Dow 30 and it was created by Dow Jones company co-founder Mr. Charles Dow. It has 30 major American companies in the index.

COMPANY	SYMBOL	INDUSTRY
1. 3M	MMM	Conglomerate
2. AT&T	T	Telecommunication
3. American Express	AXP	consumer finance

Investors get rich

COMPANY	SYMBOL	INDUSTRY
4. Boeing	BA	Defense / Aerospace
5. Coca-Cola	KO	Beverages
6. Cisco Systems	CSCO	Computer
7. Chevron	CVX	Oil and Gas
8. Caterpillar	CAT	Construction/mining
9. DuPont	DD	Chemical
10. Exxon Mobil	XOM	Oil and Gas
11. Goldman Sachs	GS	Banking
12. General Electric	GE	conglomerate
13. The Home Depot	HD	Retail
14. Intel	INTC	Semiconductors
15. IBM	IBM	Computer
16. J P Morgan Chase	JPM	Banking
17. Johnson &Johnson	JNJ	Pharmaceuticals
18. Microsoft	MSFT	Software
19. Merck	MRK	Pharmaceuticals
20. McDonalds	MCD	Food
21. Nike	NKE	Apparel
22. Procter &Gamble	PG	Consumer Goods
23. Pfizer	PFE	Pharmaceuticals
24. Travelers	TRV	Insurance
25. United Technologies	UTX	Conglomerate
26. United Health Group	UNH	Health care
27. Visa	V	Banking
28. Verizon	VZ	Telecommunication
29. Wal-Mart	WMT	Retail
30. Walt Disney	DIS	Entertainment

Basker Selwyn

S&P 500 INDEX

The S&P 500 is considered as an important indicator of the United States economy. It is one of the most popular index followed by investors. The index has 500 large capitalized companies that are listed on the New York Stock Exchange or NASDAQ.

COMPANY	SYMBOL	SECTOR
1. AbbVie	ABBV	Health Care
2. Abbott Laboratories	ABT	Health Care
3. ACE Limited	ACE	Financials
4. Accenture Plc	ACN	Information Tech
5. Actavis Plc	ACT	Pharmaceuticals
6. Adobe Systems	ADBE	Information Tech
7. ADT Corp	ADT	Comm.Service
8. AES Corp	AES	Utilities
9. Aetna Inc.	AET	Health Care
10. Aflac Inc.	AFL	Financials
11. Affiliated Managers Group	AMG	Financials
12. Agilient Technologies	A	Health Care
13. AGL Resources Inc.	GAS	Utilities
14. Air Products & Chemicals	APD	Materials

Investors get rich

COMPANY	SYMBOL	SECTOR
15. Airgas Inc.	ARG	Materials
16. Akamai Technologies	AKAM	Information Tech.
17. Alcoa Inc.	AA	Materials
18. Alexion Pharmaceuticals	ALXN	Biotechnology
19. Allegheny Technologies	ATI	Materials
20. Allegion	ALLE	Industrials
21. Allergan Inc.	AGN	Health care
22. Alliance Data Systems	ADS	Information Tech.
23. Allstate Corp	ALL	Financials
24. Altria Group Inc.	MO	Tobacco
25. Alteria Corp	ALTR	Information Tech.
26. Amazon.com Inc.	AMZN	Consumer Disc.
27. Ameren Corp	AEE	Utilities
28. American Electric Power	AEP	Utilities
29. American Express co.	AXP	Financials
30. American International Group	AIG	Financials
31. American Tower Corp.	AMT	Financials
32. Ameriprise Financials	AMP	Financials
33. Amerisource Bergen Cor.	ABC	Health Care
34. Ametek	AME	Industrials
35. Amgen Inc.	AMGN	Health Care
36. Amphenol Corp.	APH	Industrials
37. Anadarko Petroleum Corp.	APC	Energy
38. Analog Device Inc.	ADI	Information Tech.
39. Aon Plc	AON	Financials
40. Apache Corporation	APA	Energy

Basker Selwyn

COMPANY	SYMBOL	INDUSTRY
41. Apartment Investment and Management	AIV	Financials
42. Apple Inc.	AAPL	Information Tech.
43. Applied Materials Inc.	AMAT	Information Tech.
44. Archer Daniels Midland	ADM	Consumer Staples
45. Assurant Inc.	AIZ	Financials
46. AT&T Inc.	T	Telecom.
47. Autodesk Inc.	ADSK	Information Tech.
48. Automatic Data Processing	ADP	Information Tech.
49. AutoNation Inc.	AN	Consumer Disc.
50, AutoZone Inc.	AZO	Consumer disc.
51. Avago Technologies	AVGO	Information Tech.
52. Avalon Bay communities	AVB	Financials
53. Avery Dennison Corp	AVP	Materials
54. Avon Products	AVP	Consumer Staples
55. Baker Hughes Inc.	BHI	Energy
56. Ball Corp.	BLL	Materials
57. Bank of America Corp.	BAC	Financials
58. Baxter International Inc.	BAX	Health Care
59. Bank of New York	BK	Financials
60. CR Bard Inc.	BCR	Health Care

Investors get rich

COMPANY	SYMBOL	SECTOR
61. BB&T Corp	BBT	Financials
62. Becton Dickinson	BDX	Health Care
63. Bed Bath &Beyond	BBBY	Consumer Disc.
64. Bemis company	BMS	Materials
65. Berkshire Hathaway	BRK.B	Financials
66. Best Buy Co. Inc.	BBY	Consumer Disc.
67. Biogen Idec Inc.	BIIB	Health Care
68. Black Rock	BLK	Financials
69. Boeing Company	BA	Industrials
70. Borgwarner	BWA	Consumer Disc.
71. Boston scientific	BSX	Health Care
72. Boston Properties	BXP	Financials
73. Bristol-Myers squibb	BMY	Health Care
74. Broadcom Corp.	BRCM	Information Tech.
75. Brown forman Corp	BFB	Consumer Staples
76. C.H.Robinson Worldwide	CHRW	Industrials
77. CA Inc.	CA	Information Tech.
78. Cablevision Systems	CVC	Consumer Disc.
79. Cabot Oil &Gas	COG	Energy
80. Cameron International	CAM	Energy
81. Campbell soup	CPB	Consumer Staples
82. Capital One Financial	COF	Financials
83. Cardinal Health	CAH	Health Care
84. Carefusion	CFN	Health Care
85. Carmax Inc.	KMX	Consumer Disc.

COMPANY	SYMBOL	SECTOR
86. Carnival Corp.	CCL	Consumer Disc.
87. Caterpillar Inc.	CAT	Industrials
88. CBRE Group	CBG	Financials
89. CBS Corp.	CBS	Consumer Disc.
90. Celgene Corp.	CELG	Health Care
91. Center Point Energy	CNP	Utilities
92. CenturyLink Inc.	CTL	Telecom.
93. Cerner	CERN	Health Care
94. CF Industries Holdings Inc.	CF	Materials
95. Charles Schwab	SCHW	Financials
96. Chesapeake Energy	CHK	Energy
97. Chevron Corp.	CVX	Energy
98. Chipotle Mexican Grill	CMG	Restaurants
99. Chubb Corp.	CB	Financials
100. Cigna Corp	CI	Health Care
101. Cimarex Energy	XEC	Energy
102. Cincinnati financial	CINF	Financial
103. Cintas Corporation	CTA	Industrials
104. Cisco Systems	CSCO	Information Tech.
105. Citigroup	C	Financials

Investors get rich

COMPANY	SYMBOL	SECTOR
106. Citrix Systems	CTXS	Information Tech.
107. The Clorox Company	CLX	Consumer Staples
108. CME Group Inc.	CME	Financials
109. CMS energy	CMS	Utilities
110. Coach Inc.	COH	Consumer disc.
111. The Coca Cola company	KO	Consumer Staples
112. Coca-Cola Enterprises	CCE	Consumer Staples
113. Cognizant Technology Solutions	CTSH	Information Tech.
114. Colgate Palmolive	CL	Consumer Staples
115. Comcast Corp.	CMCSA	Consumer disc.
116. Comerica Inc.	CMA	Financials
117. Computer Sciences Corp.	CSC	Information Tech.
118. Con Agra Foods Inc.	CAG	Consumer Staples
119. ConocoPhillips	COP	Energy
120. Consol Energy Inc.	CNX	Energy
121. Consolidated Edison	ED	Utilities
122. Constellation Brands	STZ	Consumer Staples
123. Corning Inc.	GLW	Industrials
124. Costco Co.	COST	Consumer Staples
125. Covidien Plc	COV	Health Care
126. Crown Castle International	CCI	Financials
127. CSX Corp.	CSX	Industrials
128. Cummins Inc.	CMI	Industrials
129. CVS Caremark Corp.	CVS	Consumer Staples
130. D.R.Horton	DH	Consumer Disc.

COMPANY	SYMBOL	SECTOR
131. Danaher Corp.	DHR	Industrials
132. Darden Restaurants	DRI	Consumer Disc.
133. DaVita Inc.	DVA	Health Care
134. Deere &Co	DE	Industrials
135. Delphi Automobile	DLPH	Consumer Disc.
136. Delta Air Lines	DAL	Industrials
137. Denbury Resources	DNR	Energy
138. Dentsply International	XRAY	Health Care
139. Devon Energy Corp.	DVN	Energy
140. Diamond Offshore Drilling	D	Energy
141. DirecTV	DT	Consumer Disc.
142. Discover financial services	DFS	Financials
143. Discovery Communications -A	DISCA	Consumer Disc.
144. Discovery Communications-C	DISCK	Consume Disc.
145. Dollar General	DG	Consumer Disc.
146. Dollar Tree	DLTR	Consumer Disc.

Investors get rich

COMPANY	SYMBOL	SECTOR
147. Dominion Resources	D	Utilities
148. Dover Corp.	DOV	Industrials
149. Dow Chemical	DOW	Materials
150. Dr. Pepper Snapple Group	DPS	Consumer Staples
151. DTE Energy Co.	DTE	Utilities
152. DuPont	DD	Materials
153. Duke Energy	DUK	Utilities
154. Dun &Bradstreet	DNB	Industries
155. E-Trade	ETFC	Financials
156. Eastman Chemical	EMN	Materials
157. Eaton Corporation	ETN	Industrials
158. eBay Inc.	EBAY	Information Tech.
159. Ecolab Inc.	ECL	Materials
160. Edison International	EIX	Utilities
161. Edwards Life sciences	EW	Health Care
162. Electronic Arts	EA	Information Tech.
163. EMC Corp.	EMC	Information Tech.
164. Emerson Electric	EMR	Industrials
165. Ensco plc	ESV	Energy
166. Entergy Corp.	ETR	Utilities
167. EOG Resources	EOG	Energy
168. EQT Corporation	EQT	Energy
169. Equifax Inc.	EFX	Financials
170. Equity Residential	EQR	Financials

COMPANY	SYMBOL	SECTOR
171. Essex Property Trust Inc.	ESS	Financials
172. Estee Lauder Cos.	EL	Consumer Staples
173. Exelon Corp.	EXC	Utilities
174. Expedia Inc.	EXPE	Consumer Disc.
175. Expeditors Int'l of Washington	EXPD	Industrials
176. Express Scripts	ESRX	Health Care
177. Exxon Mobil Corp.	XOM	Energy
178. F5 Networks	FFIV	Information Tech.
179. Facebook	FB	Information Tech.
180. Family Dollar stores	FDO	Consumer Disc.
181. Fastenal Co.	FAST	Industrials
182. FedEx Corporation	FDX	Industrials
183. Fidelity National Information services	FIS	Information Tech.
184. Fifth Third Bancorp	FITB	Financials
185. First solar Inc.	FSLR	Energy
186. First Energy corp.	FE	Utilities
187. Fiserv Inc.	FISV	Information Tech.
188. FLIR Systems	FLIR	Industrials
189. Flowserve Corporation	FLS	Industrials
190. Fluor Corp.	FLR	Industrials
191. FMC Corporation	FMC	Materials
192. FMC Technologies Inc.	FTI	Energy

Investors get rich

COMPANY	SYMBOL	SECTOR
193. Ford Motor	F	Consumer Disc.
194. Fossil Inc.	FOSL	Consumer Disc.
195. Franklin Resources	BEN	Financials
196. Freeport McMoran Inc.	FCX	Materials
197. Frontier communications	FTR	Telecom.
198. GameStop Corp.	GME	Consumer Disc.
199. Gannett Co.	GCI	Consumer Disc.
200. The Gap Inc.	GPS	Consumer Disc.
201. Garmin Ltd.	GRMN	Consumer Disc.
202. General Dynamics	GD	Industrials
203. General Electric	GE	Industrials
204. General Growth Properties Inc.	GGP	Financials
205. General Mills	GIS	Consumer Staples
206. General Motors	GM	Consumer Disc.
207. Genuine Parts	GPC	Consumer Disc.
208. Genworth financial Inc.	GN	Financials
209. Gilead Sciences	GILD	Health Care
210. Goldman Sachs Group	GS	Financials
211. Goodyear Tire & Rubber	GT	Consumer Disc.
212. Google Inc. Class A	GOOGL	Information Tech.
213. Google Inc. Class C	GOOG	Information Tech.
214. W.W. Grainger Inc.	GWW	Industrials
215. Halliburton Co.	HAL	Energy

COMPANY	SYMBOL	SECTOR
216. H&R Block Inc.	HRB	Services
217. Harley Davidson	HOG	Consumer Disc.
218. Harman Int'l Industries	HAR	Consumer Disc.
219. Harris Corporation	HRS	Information Tech.
220. Hartford Financial Services	HIG	Financials
221. Hasbro Inc.	HAS	Consumer Disc.
222. HCP Inc.	HCP	Financials
223. Health care REIT Inc.	HCN	Financials
224. Helmerich &Payne	HP	Energy
225. Hess Corporation	HES	Energy
226. Hewlett Packard	HPQ	Information Tech.
227. Home Depot	HD	Consumer Disc.
228. Honeywell Int'l Inc.	HON	Industrials
229. Hormel Foods Corp	HRL	Consumer Staples
230. Hospira Inc.	HSP	Health Care
231. Host Hotels & Resorts	HST	Financials
232. Hudson city Bancorp	HCBK	Financials
233. Humana Inc.	HUM	Health Care
234. Huntington Bancshares	HBAN	Financials
235. Illinois Tool Works	ITW	Industrials

Investors get rich

COMPANY	SYMBOL	SECTOR
236. Ingersoll Rand PLC	IR	Industrials
237. Integrys Energy Group	TEG	Utilities
238. Intel Corp.	INTC	Information Tech.
239. Intercontinental Exchange	ICE	Financials
240. International Business Machines	IBM	Information Tech.
241. International Paper	IP	Materials
242. Interpublic Group	IPG	Consumer disc.
243. Int'l Flavors & Fragrances	IFF	Materials
244. Intuit Inc.	INTU	Information Tech.
245. Intuitive surgical Inc.	ISRG	Health Care
246. Invesco Ltd.	IVZ	Financials
247. Iron Mountain Incorporated	IRM	Industrials
248. Jabil circuit	JBL	Information Tech.
249. Jacobs Engineering Group	JEC	Industrials
250. Johnson & Johnson	JNJ	Health Care
251. Johnson Controls	JCI	Consumer disc.
252. Joy Global Inc.	JOY	Industrials
253. JPMorgan Chase &Co	JPM	Financials
254. Juniper Networks	JNPR	Information tech.
255. Kansas City Southern	KSU	Industrials
256. Kellogg Co.	K	Consumer staples
257. Keycorp	KEY	Financials
258. Keurig Green Mountain	GMCR	Consumer Staples
259. Kimberly Clark	KMB	Consumer Staples
260. Kimco Realty	KIM	Financials

COMPANY	SYMBOL	SECTOR
261. kinder Morgan	KMI	Energy
262. KLA Tencor Corp.	KLAC	Information Tech.
263. Kohl's Corp	KSS	Consumer Disc.
264. Kraft Foods Group	KRFT	Consumer Staples
265. Kroger Co.	KR	Consumer Staples
266. L Brands Inc.	LB	Consumer Disc.
267. L-3 Communications	LLL	Industrials
268. Laboratory Corp of America Holding	LH	Health Care
269. Lam Research	LRCX	Information Tech.
270. Legg Mason	LM	Financials
271. Leggett & Platt	LEG	Industrials
272. Lennar Corp	LEN	Consumer Disc.
273. Leucadia National Corp.	LUK	Financials
274. Eli Lilly & Co.	LLY	Health Care
275. Lincoln National	LNC	Financials
276. Linear Technology	LLTC	Information Tech.
277. Lockheed Martin Corp.	LMT	Industrials
278. Loews Corp.	L	Financials
279. Lorillard Inc.	LO	Consumer Staples
280. Lowe's Cos	LOW	Consumer Disc.

Investors get rich

COMPANY	SYMBOL	SECTOR
281. Lyondell Basell	LYB	Materials
282. M&T Bank Corp.	MTB	Financials
283. Macerich	MAC	Financials
284. Macys Inc.	M	Consumer Disc.
285. 3M Company	MMM	Industrials
286. Mallinchrodt Plc	MNK	Health Care
287. Marathon Oil Corp.	MRO	Energy
288. Marathon Petroleum	MPC	Energy
289. Marriott Int'l	MAR	Consumer Disc.
290. Marsh &McLennan	MMC	Financials
291. Masco Corp.	MAS	Industrials
292. MasterCard Inc.	MA	Information Tech.
293. Mattel Inc.	MAT	Consumer Disc.
294. McCormick & Co.	MKD	Consumer Staples
295. McDonald's Corp.	MCD	Consumer Disc.
296. McGraw Hill Financial	MHFI	Financials
297, McKesson Corp.	MCK	Health Care
298. Mead Johnson	MJN	Consumer Staples
299. MeadWestvaco Corp.	MWV	Materials
300. Medtronic Inc.	MDT	Health Care

Basker Selwyn

COMPANY	SYMBOL	SECTOR
301. Merck &Co.	MRK	Health Care
302. MetLife Inc.	MET	Financials
303. Microchip Technology	MCHP	Information Tech.
304. Micron Technology	MU	Information Tech.
305. Microsoft Corp.	MSFT	Information Tech.
306. Mohawk Industries	MHK	Consumer Disc.
307. Molson Coors Brewing	TAP	Consumer Staples
308. Mondelez International	MDLZ	Consumer Staples
309. Monsanto Co.	MON	Materials
310. Monster Beverage	MNST	Consumer Staples
311. Moody's Corp.	MCO	Financials
312. Morgan Stanley	MS	Financials
313. The Mosaic Company	MOS	Materials
314. Motorola solutions Inc.	MSI	Information Tech.
315. Murphy Oil	MUR	Energy
316. Mylan Inc.	MYL	Health Care
317. Michael Kors	KORS	Consumer disc.
318. Martin Marietta Materials	MLM	Materials
319. Nabors Industries Ltd.	NBR	Energy
320. NASDAQ OMX Group	NDAQ	financials
321. National Oil well Varco	NOV	Energy
322. Navient Corp.	NAVI	Financials

Investors get rich

COMPANY	SYMBOL	SECTOR
323. NetApp	NTAP	Information Tech.
324. Netflix Inc.	NFLX	Information Tech.
325. Newell Rubbermaid	NWL	Consumer Disc.
326. Newfield Exploration	NFX	Energy
327. Newmont Mining	NEM	Materials
328. News Corporation	NWSA	Consumer Disc.
329. Next Era Energy	NEE	Utilities
330. Nielsen Holdings	NLSN	Industrials
331. NIKE Inc.	NKE	Consumer Disc.
332. NiSource Inc.	NI	Utilities
333. Noble Corp.	NE	Energy
334. Nordstrom	JWN	Consumer Disc.
335. Norfolk Southern Corp.	NSC	Industrials
336. Northern Trust Corp.	NTRS	Financials
337. Northrop Grumman	NOC	Industrials
338. Northeast Utilities	NU	Utilities
339. NRG Energy	NRG	Utilities
340. Nucor Corp.	NUE	Materials
341. Nvidia Corporation	NVDA	Information Tech.
342. O'Reilly Automotive	ORLY	Consumer Disc.

Basker Selwyn

COMPANY	SYMBOL	SECTOR
343. Occidental Petroleum	OXY	Energy
344. Omnicom Group	OM	Consumer Disc.
345. ONEOK	OKE	Energy
346. Oracle Corp.	ORCL	Information Tech.
347. Owens Illinois Inc.	OI	Materials
348. PG&E Corp.	PCG	Utilities
349. Paccar Inc.	PCAR	Industrials
350. Pall Corp.	PLL	Industrials
351. Parker Hannifin	PH	Industrials
352. Patterson Companies	PDCO	Health Care
353. Paychex Inc.	PAYX	Information Tech.
354. Pentair Ltd.	PNR	Industrials
355, People's United Bank	PBCT	Financials
356. Pepco Holdings Inc.	POM	Utilities
357. PepsiCo Inc.	PEP	Consumer Staples
358. PerkinElmer	PKI	Health Care
359. Perrigo	PRGO	Health Care
360. PetSmart Inc.	PETM	Consumer Disc.
361. Pfizer Inc.	PFE	Health Care
362. Philip Morris Int'l	PM	Consumer Staples

Investors get rich

COMPANY	SYMBOL	SECTOR
363. Phillips 66	PSX	Energy
364. Pinnacle West Capital	PNW	Utility
365. Pioneer Natural Resources	PXD	Energy
366. Pitney Bowes	PBI	Industries
367. Plum Creek Timber	PCL	Financials
368. PNC Financial Services	PNC	Financials
369. Polo Ralph Lauren Corp	RL	Consumer Disc.
370. PPG Industries	PPG	Materials
371. PPL Corp.	PPL	Utilities
372. Praxair Inc.	PX	Materials
373. Precision Cast parts	PCP	Industrials
374. Priceline.com Inc.	PCLN	Consumer Disc.
375. Principal Financial	PFG	Financials
376. Procter & Gamble	PG	Consumer Staples
377. Progressive Corp.	PGR	Financials
378. Prologis Inc.	PLD	Financials
379. Prudential Financial	PRU	Financials
380. Public Serv. Enterprise	PEG	Utilities
381. Public Storage	PSA	Financials
382. Pulte Homes Inc.	PHM	Consumer Disc.
383. PVH Corp.	PVH	Consumer Disc.

Basker Selwyn

COMPANY	SYMBOL	SECTOR
384. QEP Resources	QEP	Energy
385. Quanta Services Inc.	PWR	Industrials
386. Qualcomm Inc.	QCOM	Information Tech.
387. Quest Diagnostics	DGX	Health Care
388. Range Resources	RRC	Energy
389. Raytheon Co.	RTN	Industrials
390. Red Hat Inc.	RHT	Information Tech.
391. Regeneron	REGN	Health Care
392. Regions Financial	RF	Financial
393. Republic Services	RSG	Industrial
394. Reynolds American	RAI	Consumer Staples
395. Robert Half Int'l	RHI	Industrials
396. Rockwell Automation	ROK	Industrials
397. Rockwell Collins	COL	Industrials
398. Roper Industries	ROP	Industrials
399. Ross Stores	ROST	Consumer Disc.
400. Ryder System	R	Industrials
401. Safeway Inc.	SWY	Consumer Staples

Investors get rich

COMPANY	SYMBOL	SECTOR
402. Salesforce.com	CRM	Information Tech.
403. SanDisk Corp.	SNDK	Information Tech.
404. SCANA Corp.	SCG	Utilities
405. Schlumberger Ltd.	SLB	Energy
406. Scripps Networks	SNI	Consumer Disc.
407. Seagate Technology	STX	Information Tech.
408. Sealed Air Corp.	SEE	Materials
409. Sempra Energy	SRE	Utilities
410. Sherwin Williams	SHW	Materials
411. Sigma Aldrich	SIAL	Materials
412. Simon Property	SPG	Financials
413. Smucker Company	SJM	Consumer Staples
414. Snap On Inc.	SNA	Consumer Disc.
415. Southern Co.	SO	Utilities
416. South West Airlines	LUV	Industries
417. South Western Energy	SWN	Energy
418. Spectra Energy Corp.	SE	Energy
419. St. Jude Medical	STJ	Health Care
420. Stanley Black & Decker	SWK	Consumer Disc.
421. Staples Inc.	SPLS	Consumer Disc.

COMPANY	SYMBOL	SECTOR
422. Starbucks Corp.	SBUX	Consumer Disc.
423. Starwood Hotels	HOT	Consumer Disc.
424. State Street Corp.	STT	Financials
425. Stericycle Inc.	SRCL	Industrials
426. Stryker Corp.	SYK	Health Care
427. SunTrust Banks	STI	Financials
428. Symantec Corp.	SYMC	Information Tech.
429. Sysco Corp .	SYY	Consumer Staples
430. T. Rowe Price Group	TROW	Financials
431. Target Corp.	TGT	Consumer Disc.
432. TE Connectivity Ltd.	TEL	Information Tech.
433. TECO Energy	TE	Utilities
434. Tenet Health Care	THC	Health Care
435. Teradata Corp.	TDC	Information Tech.
436. Tesoro Petroleum	TSO	Energy
437. Texas Instruments	TXN	Information Tech.
438. Textron Inc.	TXT	Industrials
439. The Hershey Company	HSY	Consumer Staples
440. Travelers Company	TRV	Financials
441. Thermo Fisher Scientific	TMO	Health Care

Investors get rich

COMPNAY	SYMBOL	SECTOR
442. Tiffany &Co.	TIF	Consumer Disc.
443. Time Warner Inc.	TWX	Consumer Disc.
444. TJX Companies	TJX	Consumer Disc.
445. Torchmark Corp.	TMK	Financials
446. Total System	TSS	Information Tech.
447. Tractor supply	TSCO	Consumer Disc.
448. Transocean	RIG	Energy
449. Trip Advisor	TRIP	Consumer Disc.
450. Twenty first Century fox	FOXA	Consumer Disc.
451. Tyson Foods	TSN	Consumer Staples
452. Tyco International	TYC	Industrials
453. U.S. Bancorp	USB	Financials
454. Under Armour	UA	Consumer Disc.
455. Union Pacific	UNP	Industrials
456. United Health Group	UNH	Health Care
457. United Parcel Service	UPS	Industrials
458. United Rentals	URI	Industrials
459. United technologies	UTX	Industrials
460. Universal Health	UHS	Health Care

COMPANY	SYMBOL	SECTOR
461. Unum Group	UNM	Financials
462. Urban Outfitters	URBN	Consumer Disc.
463. V.F.Corp.	VFC	Consumer Disc.
464. Valero Energy	VLO	Energy
465. Varian Medical	VAR	Health Care
466. Ventas Inc.	VTR	Financials
467. verisign Inc.	VRSN	Information Tech.
468. Verizon	VZ	Telecommunication
469. Vertex	VRTX	Health Care
470. Viacom Inc.	VIAB	Consumer Disc.
471. Visa Inc.	V	Information Tech.
472. Vornado Realty Trust	VNO	Financials
473. Vulcan Materials	VMC	Materials
474. Wal Mart Stores	WMT	Consumer Staples
475. Walgreen Co,	WAG	Consumer Staples
476. Walt Disney	DIS	Consumer Disc.
477. Waste Management	WM	Industrials
478. Waters Corporation	WAT	Health Care
479. WellPoint Inc.	WLP	Health Care
480. Wells Fargo	WFC	Financials

Investors get rich

COMPANY	SYMBOL	SECTOR
481. Western Digital	WDC	Information Tech.
482. Western Union Co.	WU	Information Tech.
483. Weyerhaeuser Corp.	WY	Financials
484. Whirlpool Corp.	WHR	Consumer Disc.
485. Whole Foods Market	WFM	Consumer Staples
486. Williams Co.	WMB	Energy
487. Windstream Communications	WIN	Telecommunications
488. Wisconsin Energy	WEC	Utilities
489. Wyndham Worldwide	WYN	Consumer Disc.
490. Wynn Resorts	WYNN	Consumer Disc.
491. Xcel energy	XEL	Utilities
492. Xerox Corp.	XRX	Information Tech.
493. Xilinx Inc.	XLNX	Information Tech.
494. XL Capital	XL	Financials
495. Xylem Inc.	XYL	Industrials
496. Yahoo Inc.	YHOO	Information Tech.
497. Yum! Brands Inc.	Yum	Consumer Disc.
498. Zimmer Holdings	ZMH	Health Care
499. Zions Bancorp	ZION	Financials
500. Zoetis	ZTS	Health Care

Basker Selwyn

NASDAQ COMPOSITE INDEX

The Nasdaq Composite Is an index of the technology stocks listed on the Nasdaq stock market. The index has more than 3000 stocks. It is one of the few indicators for the economy of the country.

NASDAQ 100 STOCK INDEX

The Nasdaq 100 stock index consists of 100 large non-financial stocks listed on the Nasdaq stock market. It has both domestic and international stocks listed on it. The following is the Nasdaq 100 stocks listed in alphabetical order.

COMPANY	SYMBOL
1. Apple Inc.	AAPL
2. Analog Devices Inc.	ADI
3. Adobe Systems Inc.	ADBE
4. Automatic Data Processing	ADP
5. Autodesk Inc.	ADSK

Investors get rich

COMPANY	SYMBOL
6. Akamai Technologies Inc.	AKAM
7. Altera Corp.	ALTR
8. Alexion Pharmaceuticals Inc.	ALXN
9. Applied Materials Inc.	AMAT
10. Amgen Inc.	AMGN
11. Amazon.com Inc.	AMZN
12. Activision Blizzard Inc.	ATVI
13. Avago Technologies Ltd.	AVGO
14. Bed Bath & Beyond Inc.	BBBY
15. Baidu Inc.	BIDU
16. Biogen Idec Inc.	BIIB
17. Broadcom corp.	BRCM
18. CA Technologies Inc.	CA
19. Cerner Corp.	CERN
20. Celgene Corporation	CELG
21. Check Point Software Tech.	CHKP
22. CH Robinson Worldwide Inc.	CHRW
23. Charter communications	CHTR
24. Comcast Corporation	CMCSA
25. Costco Wholesale	COST
26. Cisco Systems	CSCO
27. Catamaran Corporation	CTRX
28. Citrix systems Inc.	CTXS
29. Cognizant Technology Solutions	CTSH
30. Discovery Communications	DISCK

COMPANY	SYMBOL
31. Discovery Communications	DISCA
32. Dish Network Corp.	DISH
33. Dollar Tree Inc.	DLTR
34. DIRECTV	DTV
35. eBay Inc.	EBAY
36. Express Scripts Holding Co.	ESRX
37. Equinix Inc.	EQIX
38. Expeditors Int'l of Washington	EXPD
39. Expedia Inc.	EXPE
40. Fastenal Company	FAST
41. Facebook Inc.	FB
42. F5 Networks Inc.	FFIV
43. Fiserv Inc.	FISV
44. Gilead Sciences Inc.	GILD
45. Google Inc.	GOOG
46. Google Inc.	GOOGL
47. Garmin Ltd.	GRMN
48. Henry Schein Inc.	HSIC
49. Illumina Inc.	ILMN
50. Intuit Inc.	INTU

Investors get rich

COMPANY	SYMBOL
51. Intel corporation	INTC
52. Intuitive surgical Inc.	ISRG
53. Keurig Green Mountain	GMCR
54. KLA-Tencor Corp.	KLAC
55. Kraft Foods Group	KRFT
56. Liberty global Plc	LBTYA
57. Linear Technology	LLTC
58. Liberty Interactive Corp.	LINTA
59. Liberty Media Corp.	LMCA
60. Liberty Media Corp.	LMCK
61. Marriott International Inc.	MAR
62. Mattel Inc.	MAT
63. Mondelez International Inc.	MDLZ
64. Micron Technology Inc.	MU
65. Monster Beverage Corp.	MNST
66. Microsoft Corp.	MSFT
67. Maxim Integrated Products	MXIM
68. Mylan Inc.	MYL
69. Netflix Inc.	NFLX
70. NetApp Inc.	NTAP
71. NVIDIA Corp.	NVDA
72. NXP Semiconductors	NXPI
73. O'Reilly Automotive Inc.	ORLY

COMPANY	SYMBOL
74. Paychex Inc.	PAYX
75. Paccar Inc.	PCAR
76. Qualcomm Incorporated	QCOM
77. Regeneron Pharmaceuticals	REGN
78. Ross Stores Inc.	ROST
79. SBA Communications Corp.	SBAC
80. Starbucks Corp.	SBUX
81. Sigma Aldrich Corp.	SIAL
82. Sirius XM Holdings	SIRI
83. SanDisk Corp.	SNDK
84. Staples Inc.	SPLS
85. Stericycle Inc.	SRCL
86. Seagate Technology Public Ltd.	STX
87. Symantec Corp.	SYMC
88. Trip Advisor Inc.	TRIP
89. Twenty first Century FOX Inc.	FOXA
90. The Priceline group	PCLN

Investors get rich

COMPANY	SYMBOL
91. Tractor Supply Company	TSCO
92. Tesla Motors	TSLA
93. Texas Instruments Inc.	TXN
94. Viacom Inc.	VIAB
95. VimpelCom Ltd.	VIP
96. Vodafone Group PLC	VOD
97. verisk Analytics Inc.	VRSK
98. Vertex Pharmaceuticals	VRTX
99. Western digital Corporation	WDC
100. Whole foods Market Inc.	WFM
101. Wynn Resorts Ltd.	WYNN
102. Xilinx Inc.	XLNX
103. Yahoo Inc.	YHOO

Basker Selwyn

STOCK BROKERAGE FIRMS IN THE UNITED STATES

A Stock brokerage firm is a broker that processes the buying and selling of stocks between buyers and sellers. Investors should choose between many brokerage firms according to their needs.
There are mainly two types of stock brokerage firms in the United States.

1)Full Service Stock Brokerage Firms

2) Discount Stock Brokerage Firm

FULL SERVICE STOCK BROKERAGE FIRMS

Full service stock brokerage firms provide clients investment advice and they do research for their clients.

Investors get rich

Full Service Stock Brokers work according to the clients' investment objective. They charge high commissions for their extended services.

The following are some of the main full service brokerage firms in the United States. The names of the firms are listed alphabetically.

1. Ameriprise Financial

2. AXA Advisors LLC

3. Charles Schwab &Co.

4. Chase Investment Services

5. Citigroup

6. Edward Jones

7. Fidelity Investments

8. LPL Financial

Basker Selwyn

9. Merrill Lynch Wealth Management

10. Morgan Stanley Wealth Management

11. Northwestern Mutual

12. RBC Wealth Management

13. Raymond James

14. UBS Financial Services

15. Wells Fargo Advisors

Investors get rich

DISCOUNT STOCK BROKERAGE FIRMS

The Discount Stock Brokers let their customer trade online.
They usually do not provide investment advice as much as the full service brokers do.

The Discount Stock Brokers charge lower commissions.

The following are the main Discount Brokerage Firms in the United States. The names are listed alphabetically.

1. Charles Schwab

2. E Trade

3. Fidelity

4. Firstrade Securities

5. Interactive Brokers

6. Lightspeed Web Trader

7. Merrill Edge

8. OptionsXpress

9. Scottrade

10. Sharebuilder

11. Sogo Trade

12. TD Ameritrade

13. Tradeking

14. Tradestation

15. USAA

16. Vanguard

17. Wells Fargo

18. Zions Direct

Investors get rich

STOCK MARKET IN THE YEAR 2015

CONCLUSION

As I mentioned before, this book is written for long term investors in the stock market. There is always a risk in investing in any kind of investment like stocks, bonds real estate, businesses and commodities. But if the investors invest in the right time and have patients and discipline they can get financial gain.

I cannot tell where the stock market will be tomorrow (up or Down). I can't tell where the market will be in the next week. Even I will not be able to predict where the market will be going in the next month. But what I can tell is the general trend for the stock market in the United States for the year 2015 is up.

The bull market started March 2009 and it is still continuing . Both Dow Jones Industrial average and S&P 500 are in record territories. The indexes are making new highs in the year 2014. The long term trend for the stock market in the United States is up for the year 2015. I cannot even tell which months the market will go up.

Basker Selwyn

There is going to be short term corrections in the market. We do not know what months the correction will be.

The investors should watch for Federal Monetary Policy changes like economic stimulus packages and the interest rate. If there is a drastic change in the policies it will affect the stock market.

The Investors should watch for the domestic (within the United States) and foreign political events such as war and terrorist incidents. It leads to economic turmoil and affect the stock market.

The investors should have an eye on the current events like Ebola virus. It causes uncertainty for the market and the stocks go down.

Investors get rich

The investors should look for any natural disasters domestic and globally. If anything happens like earth quake or hurricane the economy will decline and the stock market will fall. For example the great East Japan Earthquake hit Japan on the March11th 2011. The stock prices dropped sharply the following weeks.

Investors should watch different sectors. They should watch what the different sectors are doing. Especially the investors should watch for the Technology sector.

Investors also should look for the different economic indicators like Gross Domestic Product, Money supply, New and existing home sales report, jobless claims report the interest rate and the other economic indicators mentioned in this book.

Analyzing the different economic indicators for now the Stock market is in uptrend for the year 2015 in the United States.

Good luck to you all investors.

www.ingramcontent.com/pod-product-compliance
Lightning Source LLC
Chambersburg PA
CBHW071805170526
45167CB00003B/1173